MW00900450

MY MONEY MATTERS

52-Week
Money Management
Workbook for Teens and Young Adults
(ideal for young people with a job or
living away from home)

Content by LaKesha Womack

Cover Design by Mark Bailey, Yellow Dogg Designs

THIS BOOK IS DEDICATED TO ALL OF THE YOUNG PEOPLE
WITH A DESIRE TO CREATE GOOD MONEY HABITS.

IF IT TAKES 21 DAYS TO CREATE A HABIT…
THIS IS GOING TO BE A GREAT YEAR!

Copyright © 2012 LaKesha Womack

This publication is for informational purposes. It is sold with the understanding that the writer is not engaged in rendering legal, accounting or financial services. If financial advice or other expert assistance is required, the service of a competent professional person should be sought.

ISBN: 1475262957
ISBN-13: 978-1475262957

HOW TO USE THIS BOOK...

- Each week you should plan to spend at least one hour reviewing your budget from last week, working on the money principle and creating your budget for the upcoming week

- If the terms seem too complex for you to understand, ask an adult to help you or do some additional research online

- Begin each week on the same day throughout the book for consistency

GOALS...

1. To teach you the Basic Money Management Principle (weeks 1-13)

2. To encourage you to save money for your future (weeks 14-26)

3. To develop a basic understanding of financial terms (weeks 27-39)

4. To promote a legacy of investing (weeks 40-52)

Let's get started!

WEEK 1

How do I figure out which numbers to use each week?

1. Enter the month and day of the week at the top of the page each week

MONTH	SUN	MON	TUES	WED	THURS	FRI	SAT
JUNE	7	8	9	10	11	12	13

2. Count how much money have on the 7th. This should be the same amount that you ended last week with.

   I started this week with $111.50

3. Calculate how much you plan to earn between the 7th and 13th

DATE	MONEY EARNED (INCOME)	HOW MUCH
7	Allowance from parents	$25.00
13	Part Time Job	$134.00
TOTAL EARNED THIS WEEK		$159.00

4. Calculate how much you plan to spend between the 7th and 13th

DATE	MONEY SPENT	HOW MUCH
7	Save	$16.00
9	Cell Phone	$50.00
12	Movies and McDonalds	$20.00
TOTAL SPENT THIS WEEK		$86.00

5. Calculate how much money you should have on the 13th This will be the amount that you start next week with.

   This week I should have $184.50

   (I had $111.50 + I earned $159.00 – I spent $86.00)

6. Before you start planning for the next week, the 14th – 20th, review the numbers from this week to see if you stuck with your budget, if not make the corrections so that the amount you have beginning on the 14th matches how much you actually have. This includes cash and money that you have in your banking account but not savings.

MY MONEY MATTERS

MONTH	SUN	MON	TUES	WED	THURS	FRI	SAT

DATE	MONEY EARNED (INCOME)	HOW MUCH
		$
		$
		$
		$
TOTAL EARNED THIS WEEK		$

DATE	MONEY SPENT (EXPENSES)	HOW MUCH
	SAVE	$
		$
		$
		$
		$
		$
		$
		$
TOTAL SPENT THIS WEEK		$

I started this week with $_____

This week I should have $_____ (started + earned – spent)

WEEK 2

What is the Basic Money Management Principle?

The Basic Money Management Principle proclaims, "I will not spend more than I earn."

The average American spends their lifetime living from one week to the next because they spend more money than they make. When they do, three things happen…

1. **They are not able to save money** because there is not enough money left over each week to set any aside. When an emergency occurs, they don't have the money to pay for it and end up taking out loans or using credit cards which creates more debt.
2. **Some of their bills are not paid on time**, if at all. This leads to bad credit and the inability to get more credit. If you have a history of not paying your bills on time then you are not able to get loans or open credit card accounts.
3. **They are not able to buy the things that they want.** When you have a limited amount of money coming in and a lot of money going out; most people have to spend the money on the things they need and usually don't have money left for the things that they want.

The goal of this workbook is to teach you how to create money values based on saving, investing and planning for your future so that you can save money, have a habit of paying your bills on time and be able to afford some of your wants.

What is your goal for using this money management workbook?

_____

_____

_____

MONTH	SUN	MON	TUES	WED	THURS	FRI	SAT

DATE	MONEY EARNED (INCOME)	HOW MUCH
		$
		$
		$
		$
TOTAL EARNED THIS WEEK		$

DATE	MONEY SPENT (EXPENSES)	HOW MUCH
	SAVE	$
		$
		$
		$
		$
		$
		$
		$
TOTAL SPENT THIS WEEK		$

I started this week with $_____

This week I should have $_____ (started + earned – spent)

WEEK 3

What should I do if I spend more money than I receive?

So far you have been tracking your income and expenses for two weeks. Hopefully, you are not spending more money than you are making.

What happens if you do?

There will be some weeks when you need to spend more money than you make. That is why it is important to budget your money and not spend your money as soon as you make it. You want to be sure that the things you spend your money on are things that you really want so that you don't regret it later.

If you find while working through this workbook that you are not able to save any money and keep spending more than is coming in; you should consider two things…

1. **Find a way to earn more money** (for example – if you have a job, consider working a few extra hours if it will not interfere with your other obligations)
2. **Begin spending less money** – you are living outside of your weekly budget and that is a bad money habit, look at the things you are spending your money on and ask yourself if you really need them

List two ways that you can earn more money

1. _____

2. _____

List two ways that you can spend less money

1. _____

2. _____

MONTH	SUN	MON	TUES	WED	THURS	FRI	SAT

DATE	MONEY EARNED (INCOME)	HOW MUCH
		$
		$
		$
		$
TOTAL EARNED THIS WEEK		$

DATE	MONEY SPENT (EXPENSES)	HOW MUCH
	SAVE	$
		$
		$
		$
		$
		$
		$
		$
TOTAL SPENT THIS WEEK		$

I started this week with $_____

This week I should have $_____ (started + earned – spent)

WEEK 4

What is the difference between a want and a need?

It makes us sad to know that there are no money trees growing in our backyards. As you are starting to see, there are only a few dollars coming in each week to spend on the things that we want and need. To manage our budget, we have to know the difference between a want and a need. Now that you are taking control of your budget and developing smart money habits, you want to be sure that you are being responsible with your money. One way that you can do this is by knowing the difference between a want and a need then taking that into consideration when deciding how to spend your money each week.

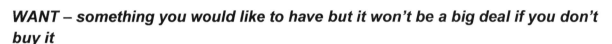

WANT – something you would like to have but it won't be a big deal if you don't buy it

NEED – something that you have to have because it is a part of maintaining your home, health or contributes to your future goals

When working on your budget each week, you should make sure that the things you **need** are taken care of before the things that you **want**.

For example, supplies for school and clothes for work are considered needs while vacations and hanging out with friends are considered wants.

List three things that you consider needs

1. _____

2. _____

3. _____

List three things that you consider wants

1. _____

2. _____

3. _____

Do you spend more of your money on wants or needs? _____

MONTH	SUN	MON	TUES	WED	THURS	FRI	SAT

DATE	MONEY EARNED (INCOME)	HOW MUCH
		$
		$
		$
		$
TOTAL EARNED THIS WEEK		$

DATE	MONEY SPENT (EXPENSES)	HOW MUCH
	SAVE	$
		$
		$
		$
		$
		$
		$
		$
TOTAL SPENT THIS WEEK		$

I started this week with $_____

This week I should have $_____ (started + earned – spent)

WEEK 5

Why is it important to save?

_____

_____

_____

It is important to save for two reasons...

1. **Rainy days** – not the days that it really rains outside but those days that something important happens and you don't have enough money to pay for it. Becoming financially independent means that you are able to take care of yourself without having to ask others for money. Without having money set aside, when an emergency occurs, like your car breaks down, you should have money set aside to pay for it because you may not earn enough money that week to pay for it out of your budget. If you don't have the money, you will have to charge it on a credit card or get a loan.

2. **To achieve your goals** – later in the workbook we will begin to talk about some of the goals that you have, the money that you save will be one of the ways that you can make those goals come true. Without having that money, some of your goals may remain a dream and you will become one of those people who think "what if" when imaging your future. Creating a plan and saving your money will allow you to say, "One day I will..."

MONTH	SUN	MON	TUES	WED	THURS	FRI	SAT

DATE	MONEY EARNED (INCOME)	HOW MUCH
		$
		$
		$
		$
TOTAL EARNED THIS WEEK		$

DATE	MONEY SPENT (EXPENSES)	HOW MUCH
	SAVE	$
		$
		$
		$
		$
		$
		$
		$
TOTAL SPENT THIS WEEK		$

I started this week with $_____

This week I should have $_____ (started + earned – spent)

WEEK 6

How much should I save?

_____

_____

_____

Most financial professionals suggest that you save ten percent of the money that you earn. If you earn $100.00 each week, you should save $10.00 each week.

Do you want a quick way to figure out how much ten percent is?

Simply take the decimal and move it to the left one space. Check out the examples below…

$200.00 → move the decimal one space left = $20.00

$460.50 → move the decimal one space left = $46.50

Now you try it…

10% of $160.00 is _____

Don't forget… You should save ten percent of the money you **earn** and not of the money have left…

How will your money matters change if you start to save 10% of all of the money you earn?

_____

_____

_____

MONTH	SUN	MON	TUES	WED	THURS	FRI	SAT

DATE	MONEY EARNED (INCOME)		HOW MUCH	
			$	
			$	
			$	
			$	
TOTAL EARNED THIS WEEK			$	

DATE	MONEY SPENT (EXPENSES)		HOW MUCH	
	SAVE		$	
			$	
			$	
			$	
			$	
			$	
			$	
			$	
TOTAL SPENT THIS WEEK			$	

I started this week with $_____

This week I should have $_____ (started + earned – spent)

WEEK 7

Where should I put the money that I am saving?

At this point in your savings career (a career is something that you do long term and we are planning for you to save for a long time); you have two basic options for saving your money.

1. Put your money in a bank at home, make sure you choose a safe place that no one knows about and consider using a lock box or something that requires a key or combination to open
2. Deposit your money into a savings account at a local bank. If you are under the age of 18 then your parents may need to assist you with opening the account.

Saving your money in a bank at home is cool because you can put money in there at any time but if you have a bank account you have to go to the bank to deposit your money

Saving money at the bank will keep you from using the money on wants because you can't go to the bank at any time to get the money out which will allow you to save your money faster because there is less chance of you spending it

Saving money at home allows you to SEE your money grow but when your money is at the bank you can only see the numbers grow on the statement they give you every month

Saving money at the bank might encourage your parents, grandparents and other family members to add money to your account because they would see that you are serious about saving your money

What do you think? Would you rather save your money at home or in a bank?

_____

Why do you think this is better you?

_____

_____

MONTH	SUN	MON	TUES	WED	THURS	FRI	SAT

DATE	MONEY EARNED (INCOME)					HOW MUCH	
						$	
						$	
						$	
						$	
TOTAL EARNED THIS WEEK						$	

DATE	MONEY SPENT (EXPENSES)					HOW MUCH	
	SAVE					$	
						$	
						$	
						$	
						$	
						$	
						$	
						$	
TOTAL SPENT THIS WEEK						$	

I started this week with $_____

This week I should have $_____ (started + earned – spent)

WEEK 8

Money Break…

Throughout this book we will be talking about how important money is, why you should save it, what you can do with it and how it can help you make your goals come true but we need to stop and take a money break so that I can tell you a few very important things…

- **Money cannot buy you happiness.** No matter how much money you make or save, it will not be the root of your happiness. True happiness will come from within and being a good person. Many people say, "Money cannot buy you happiness" because even people with a lot of money have problems. If there are things in your life that stress you out, you need to deal with those issues by talking to someone but spending money on things you don't need may make you feel better for a little while but not forever.

- **Your money should not define you.** Whether you have one dollar or a million dollars, you should never allow that to be thing that people know you for. Most people who brag about how much money they have are doing it to try to make up for something about themselves they don't like. Love yourself because you are a great person and expect other people to love you for the same reason, not because of how much money you have. If you date someone or try to get someone to date you based on money, you will never know if they really care about you or if it's the money. That may be fun for a little while but eventually you will want someone who really cares about you.

- **Whenever possible, use your money to help someone else.** You can do this by donating money to an organization that you think is doing something really cool or helping someone who is in need. Be smart about helping others with your money by researching the organization and what they do with their money before making a donation and making sure that the person you are helping has a valid need. You don't want others taking advantage of your good deeds.

- **Money is not the root of evil.** The love of money is what causes people problems. When people start to think that money is more important than the people in their lives, they start to have problems. Always remember that you should love those in your life more than money. Money is a means of accomplishing your goals.

- **Learning to save your money will be one of the best lessons that you will ever learn in life.** Years from now, you will look back on these lessons and realize that being able to budget your money is a key to your success. Most adults wish they had done a better job saving their money when they were younger. It's hard to catch up when you get older so it's best to start when you are young.

MONTH	SUN	MON	TUES	WED	THURS	FRI	SAT

DATE	MONEY EARNED (INCOME)					HOW MUCH	
						$	
						$	
						$	
						$	
TOTAL EARNED THIS WEEK						$	

DATE	MONEY SPENT (EXPENSES)					HOW MUCH	
	SAVE					$	
						$	
						$	
						$	
						$	
						$	
						$	
						$	
TOTAL SPENT THIS WEEK						$	

I started this week with $_____

This week I should have $_____ **(started + earned – spent)**

WEEK 9

Did you know…

According to treasury.gov; the motto "IN GOD WE TRUST" was placed on United States coins largely because of the increased religious sentiment existing during the Civil War. Secretary of the Treasury Salmon P. Chase received many appeals from devout persons throughout the country, urging that the United States recognize the Deity on United States coins. From Treasury Department records, it appears that the first such appeal came in a letter dated November 13, 1861. It was written to Secretary Chase by Rev. M. R. Watkinson, Minister of the Gospel from Ridleyville, Pennsylvania.

Congress passed the Act of April 22, 1864. This legislation changed the composition of the one-cent coin and authorized the minting of the two-cent coin. The Mint Director was directed to develop the designs for these coins for final approval of the Secretary. "IN GOD WE TRUST" first appeared on the 1864 two-cent coin. Another Act of Congress passed on March 3, 1865. It allowed the Mint Director, with the Secretary's approval, to place the motto on all gold and silver coins that "shall admit the inscription thereon."

MONTH	SUN	MON	TUES	WED	THURS	FRI	SAT

DATE	MONEY EARNED (INCOME)	HOW MUCH
		$
		$
		$
		$
TOTAL EARNED THIS WEEK		$

DATE	MONEY SPENT (EXPENSES)	HOW MUCH
	SAVE	$
		$
		$
		$
		$
		$
		$
		$
TOTAL SPENT THIS WEEK		$

I started this week with $_____

This week I should have $_____ (started + earned – spent)

WEEK 10

Fun facts…

Which United States President is on the face of each dollar bill?

$1	George Washington
$2	Thomas Jefferson
$5	Abraham Lincoln
$10	Alexander Hamilton
$20	Andrew Jackson
$50	Ulysses S. Grant
$100	Benjamin Franklin
$500	William McKinley
$1000	Grover Cleveland
$5000	James Madison
$10,000	Salmon P. Chase
$100,000	Woodrow Wilson

The United States Treasury no longer prints and issues bills higher than $100. Most of them are now held by collectors.

MONTH	SUN	MON	TUES	WED	THURS	FRI	SAT

DATE	MONEY EARNED (INCOME)	HOW MUCH
		$
		$
		$
		$
TOTAL EARNED THIS WEEK		$

DATE	MONEY SPENT (EXPENSES)	HOW MUCH
	SAVE	$
		$
		$
		$
		$
		$
		$
		$
TOTAL SPENT THIS WEEK		$

I started this week with $_____

This week I should have $_____ (started + earned – spent)

WEEK 11

In school you have to study history and it can seem boring to some people. History is important because we have to know where we came from to know where we are going so that we don't make some of the same mistakes moving forward. This week, I want you to talk to your parents about their money matters. Ask them these three questions...

1. What is one thing that you wish your parents had taught you about money?

_____

_____

_____

2. What are your financial goals?

_____

_____

_____

3. What do you hope I will do different with my money than you did with yours?

_____

_____

_____

MONTH	SUN	MON	TUES	WED	THURS	FRI	SAT

DATE	MONEY EARNED (INCOME)	HOW MUCH
		$
		$
		$
		$
TOTAL EARNED THIS WEEK		$

DATE	MONEY SPENT (EXPENSES)	HOW MUCH
	SAVE	$
		$
		$
		$
		$
		$
		$
		$
TOTAL SPENT THIS WEEK		$

I started this week with $_____

This week I should have $_____ (started + earned – spent)

WEEK 12

We have learned a lot in the past three months about money. Think for a minute about your money matters and your parent's money matters.

In most cultures, the children within a family work and use some of their money to help their parents since their parents worked so hard to provide for them when they were younger. When you are not practicing good money habits and spending all of your money, you are not able to help others.

There may be people in your family who you see in this situation. They never have enough money to do anything and are constantly complaining about their financial situation. There are probably other people in your life who have done a good job managing their money. They are able to travel, enjoy their lives and can help others when they choose.

You are at a point in your life where you can decide which type of person you want to be. Do you want to be the one who is always complaining about their money and asking others for money? Do you want to be the person who is able to help others when they need it?

Here's the catch… Don't become an enabler… That means that you should not make it a habit of giving the same people money on a regular basis. If you find that there is a friend or family member who is constantly asking for money then you need to ask yourself if they are good managers of their money. If not, continuing to give them money will not really help them because they will not learn to be financially responsible like you. Instead, they will start to rely on you to help them. If you find yourself in this situation, don't be afraid to talk to the person and let them know that you don't mind helping them but you are not in a position to enable them.

MONTH	SUN	MON	TUES	WED	THURS	FRI	SAT

DATE	MONEY EARNED (INCOME)	HOW MUCH
		$
		$
		$
		$
TOTAL EARNED THIS WEEK		$

DATE	MONEY SPENT (EXPENSES)	HOW MUCH
	SAVE	$
		$
		$
		$
		$
		$
		$
		$
TOTAL SPENT THIS WEEK		$

I started this week with $_____

This week I should have $_____ (started + earned – spent)

WEEK 13

How do you think our society would be different if more people saved money and followed our Basic Money Management Principle?

_____

_____

_____

_____

MONTH	SUN	MON	TUES	WED	THURS	FRI	SAT

DATE	MONEY EARNED (INCOME)	HOW MUCH
		$
		$
		$
		$
TOTAL EARNED THIS WEEK		$

DATE	MONEY SPENT (EXPENSES)	HOW MUCH
	SAVE	$
		$
		$
		$
		$
		$
		$
		$
TOTAL SPENT THIS WEEK		$

I started this week with $_____

This week I should have $_____ (started + earned – spent)

YOU HAVE JUST COMPLETED PART ONE OF YOUR MONEY MATTERS

LET'S CHECK ON YOUR MONEY MATTERS...

At the beginning of week 1, I had $_____

Between weeks 1 and 13, I earned $_____

Between weeks 1 and 13, I spent $_____

I should have (had + earned – spent) $_____

I have saved $_____

THE GOAL OF THIS SECTION WAS TO LEARN THE BASIC MONEY MANAGEMENT PRINCIPLE

BREIFLY DESCRIBE WHAT YOU HAVE LEARNED ABOUT MONEY

_____

_____

_____

_____

_____

_____

_____

WEEK 14

What are goals?

In life many people have things that they want to accomplish and we often call those things goals. Goals are the plans that we make for the future. One of my favorite sayings is… "Shoot for the moon, even if you miss, you'll land among the stars."

It took me a while to figure out what that means but once I did, it changed the way I thought about setting my goals.

When you start thinking about the things that you want to accomplish in life, you should dream big. You should set big goals for yourself. You should want to be the best and at the top of whatever you chose to do.

For example, you could set the goal of graduating from college or you could set the goal of graduating with a 3.7 GPA in four years.

If you say that you want to graduate from college (the moon) but you fall short, you may graduate but what will be your GPA and how long will it take you (the stars)?. But if you say you want to graduate from college with a 3.7 GPA in four years (the moon) but fall short, then you may end up with your degree in four and a half years and a 3.5 GPA (the stars). The difference will be like taking a trip and knowing exactly where you want to go. It may take a little longer than you planned but you know where you are going and how to get there.

When you set your goals high and work hard to achieve them, you may fall short of whatever your goal is but if you set them high then you will achieve more than most people.

During this section, we will be talking about goals and how your money can help you achieve your goals. Start thinking about some of the things that you want to achieve in your life and don't forget…

DREAM BIG!!!

MONTH	SUN	MON	TUES	WED	THURS	FRI	SAT

DATE	MONEY EARNED (INCOME)	HOW MUCH
		$
		$
		$
		$
TOTAL EARNED THIS WEEK		$

DATE	MONEY SPENT (EXPENSES)	HOW MUCH
	SAVE	$
		$
		$
		$
		$
		$
		$
		$
TOTAL SPENT THIS WEEK		$

I started this week with $_____

This week I should have $_____ **(started + earned – spent)**

WEEK 15

Why do I need to have goals?

"If you believe it, you can achieve it."

Once you set your goals, you have to believe that you can achieve them. There will be days in your life that you will think it is not possible to achieve your goals. There will be days that someone may tell you that what you want to do is not possible. You have to put all of that in the back of your mind and remind yourself…

If I believe it, I can achieve it!

It could be working on your homework assignment, saving money next week, passing your next test, getting a promotion on your job… The above statement is called an affirmation. It is a positive phrase that you tell yourself when you are starting to have a negative thought about a situation. By repeating affirmations, we change our negative thoughts to positive thoughts.

There should not be any goal that you set in life that you don't believe you can achieve. To achieve your goals, you need to do three things…

1. **Write them down.** Think about what you want and write it down. When you write it down, it stops becoming a dream stuck in your head and becomes a goal for you to work toward achieving. When you see it, you start to believe it and when you believe it, you can achieve it.
2. **Prepare.** Once you set the goal, you have to start thinking about how you will make it a reality. If you want your dream job, you have to figure out what qualifications you need to get it then create a plan to become qualified. If you want to save $1,000 by the end of the year, you need to decide how much you will save each week.
3. **Just do it**. Now that you know what you want to do and have a plan to do it; you have to take action. Imagine having a goal to get a summer internship. First you should write down the goal, then you need to find some internships that you are interested in and the qualifications for those positions. Next you have to make sure you meet those qualifications and start completing the application process. It will not be enough to just think about what you want to do. Those people are called dreamers and rarely achieve their goals. You want to be a person of action which means you have to do something about making your goals a reality.

MONTH	SUN	MON	TUES	WED	THURS	FRI	SAT

DATE	MONEY EARNED (INCOME)	HOW MUCH
		$
		$
		$
		$
TOTAL EARNED THIS WEEK		$

DATE	MONEY SPENT (EXPENSES)	HOW MUCH
	SAVE	$
		$
		$
		$
		$
		$
		$
		$
TOTAL SPENT THIS WEEK		$

I started this week with $_____

This week I should have $_____ **(started + earned – spent)**

WEEK 16

How do I set SMART goals?

To help you achieve your goals, they need to be SMART…

Simple – sometimes we don't achieve our goals because we try to make things too complicated, when you set your goals, keep it simple, stay focused on the ultimate outcome that you desire

Meaningful – you will have a better chance of achieving your goal if it means something to you, you are at a point in your life where other people have probably shared their ideas of what your future should or could look like, you may agree with some of it and disagree with some, it is important when you start to think of the goals that you want to achieve for them to mean something to you

Achievable – most of us know what we are capable of and even as we dream big we have to make sure that we are setting goals that are possible for us to achieve otherwise we are setting ourselves up for failure

Results Oriented – don't forget to begin with the end in mind, when you are setting your goals, close your eyes and imagine what it will look like when you achieve it, imagine the result and create a plan to get your from where you are now to where you want to be

Trackable – throughout this workbook we will be tracking your progress toward achieving your goals, this is called being accountable, you need to check up on yourself to be sure you are doing things that will get you to the result, if not then you will have a chance to make adjustments or change your behavior

Example of a SMART goal… You want to save $300 to take a weekend trip with your friend and their family during the upcoming holiday season

It's simple – you want to save $300

It's meaningful – saving the money will allow you to enjoy the trip

It's achievable – you have enough time to save the money and you make enough to save the money

It's results oriented – the end result is having $300 set aside for the trip

It's trackable – at the end of each month leading up to the trip, you can track how much you have saved to see whether you are on track toward achieving the goal

MONTH	SUN	MON	TUES	WED	THURS	FRI	SAT

DATE	MONEY EARNED (INCOME)	HOW MUCH
		$
		$
		$
		$
TOTAL EARNED THIS WEEK		$

DATE	MONEY SPENT (EXPENSES)	HOW MUCH
	SAVE	$
		$
		$
		$
		$
		$
		$
		$
TOTAL SPENT THIS WEEK		$

I started this week with $_____

This week I should have $_____ (started + earned – spent)

WEEK 17

Since this book is all about your money matters, what is a goal that you have for the money you are saving?

_____

_____

_____

_____

_____

Let's make it a SMART goal…

My goal for my money is simple because _____

_____

My money goal is meaningful to me because _____

_____

I will achieve my money goal by _____

_____

The result of my money goal will be _____

_____

I will track my money goal by _____

_____

MONTH	SUN	MON	TUES	WED	THURS	FRI	SAT

DATE	MONEY EARNED (INCOME)	HOW MUCH
		$
		$
		$
		$
TOTAL EARNED THIS WEEK		$

DATE	MONEY SPENT (EXPENSES)	HOW MUCH
	SAVE	$
		$
		$
		$
		$
		$
		$
		$
TOTAL SPENT THIS WEEK		$

I started this week with \$_____

This week I should have \$_____ (started + earned – spent)

WEEK 18

We have talked a lot about goals and I am sure you have started to think about some goals that you want to achieve in other areas of your life. What is one thing that you want to achieve?

_____

_____

Let's make it a SMART goal…

My goal is simple because _____

_____

My goal is meaningful to me because _____

_____

I will achieve my goal by_____

_____

The result of my goal will be _____

_____

I will track my goal by _____

_____

MONTH	SUN	MON	TUES	WED	THURS	FRI	SAT

DATE	MONEY EARNED (INCOME)	HOW MUCH
		$
		$
		$
		$
TOTAL EARNED THIS WEEK		$

DATE	MONEY SPENT (EXPENSES)	HOW MUCH
	SAVE	$
		$
		$
		$
		$
		$
		$
		$
TOTAL SPENT THIS WEEK		$

I started this week with \$_____

This week I should have \$_____ (started + earned – spent)

WEEK 19

Let's think about one more goal that you have… What is it?

SMART
Specific, Measurable, Active, Realistic, and Timed
GOALS

_____
_____
_____
_____
_____

Let's make it a SMART goal…

My goal is simple because _____

_____

My goal is meaningful to me because _____

_____

I will achieve my goal by_____

_____

The result of my goal will be _____

_____

I will track my goal by _____

_____

MONTH	SUN	MON	TUES	WED	THURS	FRI	SAT

DATE	MONEY EARNED (INCOME)					HOW MUCH	
						$	
						$	
						$	
						$	
TOTAL EARNED THIS WEEK						$	

DATE	MONEY SPENT (EXPENSES)					HOW MUCH	
	SAVE					$	
						$	
						$	
						$	
						$	
						$	
						$	
						$	
TOTAL SPENT THIS WEEK						$	

I started this week with $_____

This week I should have $_____ (started + earned – spent)

WEEK 20

Money break…

How are you doing with your budget? Do you have money left over each week or do you find yourself falling short each week?

_____

_____

_____

_____

_____

How do you feel about saving your money?

_____

_____

_____

_____

_____

Other thoughts about your money matters?

_____

_____

_____

_____

MONTH	SUN	MON	TUES	WED	THURS	FRI	SAT

DATE	MONEY EARNED (INCOME)	HOW MUCH
		$
		$
		$
		$
TOTAL EARNED THIS WEEK		$

DATE	MONEY SPENT (EXPENSES)	HOW MUCH
	SAVE	$
		$
		$
		$
		$
		$
		$
		$
TOTAL SPENT THIS WEEK		$

I started this week with $_____

This week I should have $_____ (started + earned – spent)

WEEK 21

Let's take a look at how you have done saving money for the first five months…

	How much did you save during this week (look back at your worksheets)?	What is the total amount you have saved (this week + last week)?
Week 1	$	
Week 2	+ $	= $
Week 3	+ $	= $
Week 4	+ $	= $
Week 5	+ $	= $
Week 6	+ $	= $
Week 7	+ $	= $
Week 8	+ $	= $
Week 9	+ $	= $
Week 10	+ $	= $
Week 11	+ $	= $
Week 12	+ $	= $
Week 13	+ $	= $
Week 14	+ $	= $
Week 15	+ $	= $
Week 16	+ $	= $
Week 17	+ $	= $
Week 18	+ $	= $
Week 19	+ $	= $
Week 20	+ $	= $

I have saved **more** or **less** than I wanted…. _____

MONTH	SUN	MON	TUES	WED	THURS	FRI	SAT

DATE	MONEY EARNED (INCOME)	HOW MUCH
		$
		$
		$
		$
TOTAL EARNED THIS WEEK		$

DATE	MONEY SPENT (EXPENSES)	HOW MUCH
	SAVE	$
		$
		$
		$
		$
		$
		$
		$
TOTAL SPENT THIS WEEK		$

I started this week with $_____

This week I should have $_____ (started + earned – spent)

WEEK 22

It's been four months since we started working on your money matters. What do you think about the Basic Money Management Principle?

_____

_____

_____

When you receive money now, what is the first thing that you do with it?

_____

_____

_____

Has that changed since you began using this workbook?

_____

_____

_____

MONTH	SUN	MON	TUES	WED	THURS	FRI	SAT

DATE	MONEY EARNED (INCOME)	HOW MUCH
		$
		$
		$
		$
TOTAL EARNED THIS WEEK		$

DATE	MONEY SPENT (EXPENSES)	HOW MUCH
	SAVE	$
		$
		$
		$
		$
		$
		$
		$
TOTAL SPENT THIS WEEK		$

I started this week with $_____

This week I should have $_____ (started + earned – spent)

WEEK 23

Will you become a millionaire?

When I was growing up, I could not imagine having a million dollars or being considered a millionaire. I thought that was for other people, people not like me. A lot of people are like me and dream of becoming a millionaire but think that it is only a dream. They don't know that in their lifetime they will make more than a million dollars.

"It's not how much you make that counts, it's all about how much you save"

Think about this…

You start working full time at the age of 22 when you graduate from college…

You work until the age of 67 (most people in America will retire around the age of 67) which is 45 years (if you do a good job saving your money, you might be able to retire earlier)…

You earn $45,000 per year (the middle income in the United States is around $45,000, at the beginning of your career you may earn less while earning more toward the end of your career)…

$45,000.00

x 45 years

$2,025,000.00 in your lifetime

Did you realize that just doing what ordinary people do – finishing high school, going to college, getting a job, working until retirement – will earn you more than TWO MILLION DOLLARS?

"You're not worth what you make, you're worth what you save."

How much money will you have if you save ten percent of $2,025,000.00?

___

MONTH	SUN	MON	TUES	WED	THURS	FRI	SAT

DATE	MONEY EARNED (INCOME)					HOW MUCH	
						$	
						$	
						$	
						$	
TOTAL EARNED THIS WEEK						$	

DATE	MONEY SPENT (EXPENSES)					HOW MUCH	
	SAVE					$	
						$	
						$	
						$	
						$	
						$	
						$	
TOTAL SPENT THIS WEEK						$	

I started this week with $_____

This week I should have $_____ (started + earned – spent)

WEEK 24

Let's think about your future for a minute. You have already set some SMART goals but let's think long term, let's think about some long term goals.

How do you imagine your life five years from now?

_____

_____

What kind of job will you have?

_____

_____

Where will you be living?

_____

_____

What types of activities do you imagine doing with your friends and families?

_____

_____

How will saving your money help you to have the type of life that you dream of?

_____

_____

_____

MONTH	SUN	MON	TUES	WED	THURS	FRI	SAT

DATE	MONEY EARNED (INCOME)					HOW MUCH	
						$	
						$	
						$	
						$	
TOTAL EARNED THIS WEEK						$	

DATE	MONEY SPENT (EXPENSES)					HOW MUCH	
	SAVE					$	
						$	
						$	
						$	
						$	
						$	
						$	
						$	
TOTAL SPENT THIS WEEK						$	

I started this week with $_____

This week I should have $_____ (started + earned – spent)

WEEK 25

I know we have spent a lot of time talking about your goals and planning for you to achieve them.
Take a minute and ask your parents about their goals.

What three things would like they like to achieve?

1. _____

2. _____

3. _____

How will saving money help them to achieve these goals?

_____

_____

_____

_____

_____

_____

MONTH	SUN	MON	TUES	WED	THURS	FRI	SAT

DATE	MONEY EARNED (INCOME)	HOW MUCH
		$
		$
		$
		$
TOTAL EARNED THIS WEEK		$

DATE	MONEY SPENT (EXPENSES)	HOW MUCH
	SAVE	$
		$
		$
		$
		$
		$
		$
		$
TOTAL SPENT THIS WEEK		$

I started this week with $_____

This week I should have $_____ (started + earned – spent)

WEEK 26

It's been almost two months since you set your SMART goals. How's it going?

Money Goal _____

_____

_____

_____

Goal #1 _____

_____

_____

_____

Goal #2 _____

_____

_____

_____

MONTH	SUN	MON	TUES	WED	THURS	FRI	SAT

DATE	MONEY EARNED (INCOME)	HOW MUCH
		$
		$
		$
		$
TOTAL EARNED THIS WEEK		$

DATE	MONEY SPENT (EXPENSES)	HOW MUCH
	SAVE	$
		$
		$
		$
		$
		$
		$
		$
TOTAL SPENT THIS WEEK		$

I started this week with $_____

This week I should have $_____ (started + earned – spent)

YOU HAVE JUST COMPLETED PART TWO OF YOUR MONEY MATTERS

LET'S CHECK ON YOUR MONEY MATTERS…

At the beginning of week 14, I had $_____

Between weeks 14 and 26, I earned $_____

Between weeks 14 and 26, I spent $_____

I should have (had + earned – spent) $_____

I have saved $_____

	Amount I had at the beginning …	Total amount earned…	Total amount spent…	Amount I should have…	Amount Saved…
Weeks 1-13		+	-	=	
Weeks 14-26		+	-	=	+
Total					=

THE GOAL IN THIS SECTION WAS TO HELP YOU UNDERSTAND THE IMPORTANCE OF SAVING

BREIFLY DESCRIBE HOW SAVING MONEY WILL HELP YOU ACHIEVE YOUR GOALS

_____

_____

_____

_____

_____

_____

_____

WEEK 27

What is income?

The money that you earn from a job is considered income. You do a job and the person that you did the job for gives you money. Usually, the more important and specific the job is, the more money you may earn. Common jobs like fast food restaurants pay less because there are so many of them and they don't require a lot of specific skills. Jobs like designing buildings pay more money because there are not a lot of people who can do them and they require very specific skills. Most jobs will pay you more money as your skills improve. People who run major companies make a lot of money because they have a lot of responsibility and have proven that the skills they have acquired will allow them to do a good job.

As we stated earlier, the middle income in the United States is around $45,000. The jobs that you will consider for your future may pay more or less than that depending on several factors such as the amount of education that is required, the amount of experience that you should have and how many people are able to do the same job. You may notice that the job you want requires a lot of experience. There are jobs that you can do to get the experience that will lead to your dream job, like climbing a ladder.

For example, to become a Marketing Director, you may have to start out as a Marketing Assistant then move up to Marketing Manager before becoming the Marketing Director.

A High School Diploma (*may require 2 yr associate degree)	Average Annual Salary	A Bachelor's Degree (4 years)	Average Annual Salary	An Advanced Degree (2-4 additional years)	Average Annual Salary
Fast Food Worker	$15,902	Teacher	$44,718	College Professor (PhD)	$68,788
Store Clerk	$19,753	Store Manager	$29,181	Lawyer (JD)	$79,738
*Certified Nurse Assistant (CNA)	$22,152	Registered Nurse (RN)	$51,872	Family Practice Doctor (MD)	$141,950
Bank Teller	$23,562	Financial Advisor	$67,539	Certified Public Accountant (CPA)	$146,128

Source: vault.salary.com – median salaries in Montgomery AL

What is your dream job? Let's do some research… You can use a search engine like Google. Enter the job title plus the key word (salary, education, experience, etc)

My dream job _____

Pays an average of _____

Education required _____

Experience required _____

MONTH	SUN	MON	TUES	WED	THURS	FRI	SAT

DATE	MONEY EARNED (INCOME)	HOW MUCH
		$
		$
		$
		$
TOTAL EARNED THIS WEEK		$

DATE	MONEY SPENT (EXPENSES)	HOW MUCH
	SAVE	$
		$
		$
		$
		$
		$
		$
		$
TOTAL SPENT THIS WEEK		$

I started this week with $_____

This week I should have $_____ (started + earned – spent)

WEEK 28

What are bills?

I am sure you hear your parents talk about paying their bills and by now you may have a few bills of your own.   I remember growing up and being so anxious to leave home and live on my own. What I didn't realize was that living away from my parents meant that I would have to pay my own bills. As you work toward becoming financially independent, you will have to pay your own bills also. These bills are also called expenses and are the items that you enter in your "Money I Will Spend" column.

Let's see check out an example of a family's budget. Calculate how much money they have after paying each bill. The family consists of a mom, dad, son and daughter.

The mom and dad earn $2,500 per month combined	+ $2,500	
Donate 10% to church in tithes	- $250	= $2,250
Spend $500 for the house payment	- $500	= _____
Spend $100 per week on groceries	- $400	= _____
Spend $150 on lights & water	- $150	= _____
Spend $400 on car payments and car insurance	- $400	= _____
Spend $75 on the cell phone bill for family	- $75	= _____
Pay $20 minimum payments on 3 credit cards	- $60	= _____
2 kids need $10 per week for snacks & lunch at school	- $80	= _____
Mom & Dad spend $25 each per week for lunch	- $200	= _____
They have 2 cars & spend $50 per week per car on gas	- $400	= _____
They order pizza from Pizza Hut for dinner	- $25	= _____
Trip to Wal-Mart for toothpaste, tissue, etc	- $75	= _____
The family goes out to eat after church	- $60	= _____
Mom is tired and takes everyone to McDonalds	- $20	= _____

Is the family following the Basic Money Management Principle and spending less than they earn? If not, where does the extra money come from?

Now imagine something happens and either the Mom or Dad lose their job and can't go to work. The income could be cut from $2,500 to $1,250 per month. What do you think would happen to their budget?

MONTH	SUN	MON	TUES	WED	THURS	FRI	SAT

DATE	MONEY EARNED (INCOME)	HOW MUCH
		$
		$
		$
		$
TOTAL EARNED THIS WEEK		$

DATE	MONEY SPENT (EXPENSES)	HOW MUCH
	SAVE	$
		$
		$
		$
		$
		$
		$
		$
TOTAL SPENT THIS WEEK		$

I started this week with $_____

This week I should have $_____ (started + earned – spent)

WEEK 29

What is debt?

Some of the things that you will want to buy will cost more money than you have…

These things include cars and houses. Unless you do a great job of saving your money, not many people will be able to go to a car dealership and pay $45,000 from their income or savings for a car or $150,000 to the bank for a house.

In these cases, we have to get a loan. This is when we go to a company, usually a bank or credit union, and they let us borrow the money as long as we promise to pay them back. You may have gotten a loan from your parents in the past. Did you remember to pay them back or did you forget about it once you received the money and spent it? It is important for you to remember to pay back any money that someone loans you.

These loans are called debt because we now owe someone money for something that we have. Some people think that debt is a bad thing but there are some good debts and there are some bad debts.

Good debts are the ones that help us buy things we need like a house, a car or paying for college. They are good as long as we can afford to pay the money back to the company who has given it to us.

Bad debts are the ones we make for things that we want like new clothes. We can avoid bad debts by saving our money to pay for our wants instead of getting money, a loan, to pay for those things. You may be tempted to use credit to pay for some of things that you want and we will discuss why that may or may not be a good idea later. A part of the Basic Money Management Principle requires that you not spend more money than you earn and that includes using credit for wants.

Most people in our society have more debt than they can afford to pay because they used credit to buy things that they wanted and could not afford. Understanding the difference between spending money on wants and needs will help you to manage your debt.

MONTH	SUN	MON	TUES	WED	THURS	FRI	SAT

DATE	MONEY EARNED (INCOME)					HOW MUCH	
						$	
						$	
						$	
						$	
TOTAL EARNED THIS WEEK						$	

DATE	MONEY SPENT (EXPENSES)					HOW MUCH	
	SAVE					$	
						$	
						$	
						$	
						$	
						$	
						$	
						$	
TOTAL SPENT THIS WEEK						$	

I started this week with $_____

This week I should have $_____ (started + earned – spent)

WEEK 30

How do I manage my bank accounts?

By now, you may have a checking and/or savings
account. When you earn money, some of the money, if
not all, probably goes into the account and from there
you spend it on your expenses. There are three ways
that you can spend money from your account…

1. **Write a check.** A check is a document that can
    be given to someone to pay for something. Once the person has the check, they
    take it to the bank and the bank gives them money from your account. It is very
    important that you only write checks if you have money in your account. You can't
    write a check for $80 if you only have $50. The bank will either charge you a fee
    (around $35) or they will close your account.
2. **Use your debit card.** A debit card is a square plastic card that allows you to
    spend money from your account. When you go to a store and swipe your debit
    card, the store takes the money from your account. You have to keep track of how
    much money you have in your account because if you don't have enough money in
    your account then the store will decline your transaction and not allow you to buy
    your stuff.
3. **Take the money out from an ATM** (Automatic Teller Machine). Much like when
    you make a purchase at a store, you put your card into the machine and the
    machine gives you money from your account. You cannot take out more money
    than you have in your account and many of these boxes charge you to get your
    money out. Sounds strange but that is how they make money.

It is very important to monitor the balance in your account since you are probably using
your debit card for purchases, possibly writing checks and withdrawing money from an
ATM when you need cash. When you opened the account, the bank probably gave you a
little book called a transaction register. Each week when you work on your budget
worksheets, you should also be checking your transaction register to be sure that the
money you are spending from your account is being subtracted. Unlike cash, which you
can open your wallet and count, you have to check your account balance to know how
much you have in the bank. Some banks have applications that you can download for
free to your cell phone to help you monitor your account. Be careful using online
management because some transactions may take a few days to post to your account so
you may think you have more money in your account than is actually there.

MONTH	SUN	MON	TUES	WED	THURS	FRI	SAT

DATE	MONEY EARNED (INCOME)		HOW MUCH
			$
			$
			$
			$
TOTAL EARNED THIS WEEK			$

DATE	MONEY SPENT (EXPENSES)		HOW MUCH
	SAVE		$
			$
			$
			$
			$
			$
			$
			$
TOTAL SPENT THIS WEEK			$

I started this week with $_____

This week I should have $_____ **(started + earned – spent)**

WEEK 31

What is credit?

Your reputation is what people know about you. Some people have a good reputation and people think good things about them. Other people have a bad reputation and people think bad things about them. Our reputation is usually based on how we have behaved in the past. When you do bad things, people think you are bad person. But if you do good things then people will think you are good person.

Companies like banks use credit to determine your money reputation. They make these decisions based on whether you have done a good job or a bad job taking care of your money. This allows them to make decisions about whether they will let you borrow their money.

Would you want to lend money to someone who has done a bad job managing their money? If they cannot manage their own money then you will probably think it is not likely that they will do a good job managing your money. Those people are considered high risk. Banks don't like to take risks with their money. They want to be sure that if they give you some money that you will give it back plus a little extra, called interest.

Remember when we talked about getting money from a company to buy a house or a car? A company will look at your money reputation or credit to decide if they will give you money and how much money. The better job you do taking care of your money, the better your money reputation will be and the more likely you are to be able to borrow money.

Managing your debt will determine your credit reputation. Having debt and credit are not bad as long as you use them responsibly.

There are three ways that you can keep good credit…

1. Only borrow money for things that you really need
2. Only borrow an amount of money that you are sure you can pay back in a timely manner
3. Make sure you pay all of your bills BEFORE the date that they are due

MONTH	SUN	MON	TUES	WED	THURS	FRI	SAT

DATE	MONEY EARNED (INCOME)	HOW MUCH
		$
		$
		$
		$
TOTAL EARNED THIS WEEK		$

DATE	MONEY SPENT (EXPENSES)	HOW MUCH
	SAVE	$
		$
		$
		$
		$
		$
		$
		$
TOTAL SPENT THIS WEEK		$

I started this week with $_____

This week I should have $_____ (started + earned – spent)

WEEK 32

What is a credit score?

Last week we talked about credit. This week we will talk about how a company measures credit.

When you are in school and take a test or complete an assignment, the teacher gives you a grade or a score. Companies judge your money reputation using a credit score. The better your money management, the higher your credit score. The higher your credit score, the more likely you are to be able to get money from a company.

When you do a bad job managing your money, your score gets lower and the less likely you are to get money. Sometimes when people lose their job or get sick and can't work, they are not able to pay their bills which also takes points off their credit score.

Your credit score is based on the following factors…
- ✓ **35% is based on debt history**, how often you pay your bills on time; when you are late paying your bills, the company will send a report to the companies that monitor credit letting other companies know that you may not pay them on time either
- ✓ **30% is based on debt level**, how much debt you have relative to how much money you earn
- ✓ **15% is based on length of time you've been in debt**, how long you have been managing other people's money
- ✓ **10% is based on new debt**, if you are making major purchases like a new house and car, you should plan to space out the purchases so that your budget can adjust to the new payments and you can be sure that you are able to make the payments on time
- ✓ **10% is based on type of debt**, remember that there is good debt and bad debt, companies allowing you to borrow money want to know what you are spending your money on

Check out scale below to see how credit is scored…

Excellent → 800 - 850 you've done a great job paying your bills and should be able to borrow money easily

Good → 725 - 799 you may have done a few things wrong but you try to make sure your bills are paid, you should be able to borrow money if you need it

Fair → 600 - 724 you have probably had some problems paying your bills and should not try to borrow very much money right now and focus on the bills you currently have

Poor → 280 - 599 you have not done a good job managing your money and probably won't be able to borrow any money

MONTH	SUN	MON	TUES	WED	THURS	FRI	SAT

DATE	MONEY EARNED (INCOME)					HOW MUCH	
						$	
						$	
						$	
						$	
TOTAL EARNED THIS WEEK						$	

DATE	MONEY SPENT (EXPENSES)					HOW MUCH	
	SAVE					$	
						$	
						$	
						$	
						$	
						$	
						$	
						$	
TOTAL SPENT THIS WEEK						$	

I started this week with $_____

This week I should have $_____ (started + earned – spent)

WEEK 33

What is a credit card?

Credit cards allow you to buy stuff that you want and sometimes need then pay for it later. They are similar to loans except the amount you owes depends on how much you spent versus a loan which is usually for a fixed amount. A company will look at your credit and if you have done good managing your money then they will pay for what you are buying using their money with the agreement that you will pay them back for it later. They also use your credit score to decide how much money you will be able to use. The higher your credit score, the more money you are likely to be able to use.

Credit cards are good because there will be some expenses like vacations that you might not have all of the money available when you need it. They are also good if you are able to pay back all of the money that you spend on the credit card at the end of each month so that you are not accruing interest and adding debt. If you do that, you will keep having good credit because you will be showing that you are able to handle other people's money responsibly.

Credit cards are bad if you use them to buy things that you cannot afford to pay for. If you only have $30 left over at the end of each month, you should create a new bill that will cost you $50 per month. If you do this, you will end up in one of two situations. Either you won't be able to pay the bill each month or you will not be able to pay another bill. Both situations would result in you having bad credit.

Companies that give you credit make money by charging you interest on the money you get from them. Look at what happens when you charge $100 to your credit card. $100 divided by four equals $25 so the money should be paid in four months but you have to pay $30.39 more in interest, if the company is charging 10% interest each month.

	You owe	They charge 10% interest	Now you owe	You pay	Now you owe
Month 1	$100.00	+ $10.00	= $110.00	- $25.00	= $85.00
Month 2	$85.00	+ $8.50	= $93.50	- $25.00	= $68.50
Month 3	$68.50	+ $6.85	= $75.35	- $25.00	= $50.35
Month 4	$50.35	+ $5.04	= $55.39	- $25.00	= $30.39

Do you see why it is important to only use credit cards to buy things we need or to pay the $100 back at the end of the month?

MONTH	SUN	MON	TUES	WED	THURS	FRI	SAT

DATE	MONEY EARNED (INCOME)	HOW MUCH
		$
		$
		$
		$
TOTAL EARNED THIS WEEK		$

DATE	MONEY SPENT (EXPENSES)	HOW MUCH
	SAVE	$
		$
		$
		$
		$
		$
		$
		$
TOTAL SPENT THIS WEEK		$

I started this week with $_____

This week I should have $_____ (started + earned – spent)

WEEK 34

What is a charge card?

Charge cards allow you to make a purchase and pay for it when they send you a bill. There are not many companies that issue charge cards but one of the most popular is American Express®. Having an AMEX card is a big deal because there are not very many people that qualify for this level of credit.

A charge card is usually given to people with Excellent credit because the company has looked at your money reputation and decided that you are able to pay back the money they give you during the month, at the end of the month. The company trusts you a lot. By paying the money back at the end of the month, the company usually does not charge interest. These cards also come with special benefits or perks for being such a loyal customer.

The $100 that you spent on your credit card could cost you much more if you take a few months to give the company their money back but if you use a charge card, you pay the $100 back at the end of the month.

What do you think about credit cards and charge cards?

_____

_____

_____

_____

MONTH	SUN	MON	TUES	WED	THURS	FRI	SAT

DATE	MONEY EARNED (INCOME)					HOW MUCH	
						$	
						$	
						$	
						$	
TOTAL EARNED THIS WEEK						$	

DATE	MONEY SPENT (EXPENSES)					HOW MUCH	
	SAVE					$	
						$	
						$	
						$	
						$	
						$	
						$	
						$	
TOTAL SPENT THIS WEEK						$	

I started this week with $_____

This week I should have $_____ (started + earned – spent)

WEEK 35

What are prepaid cards?

Some people who do not have good credit are not able to open checking/savings accounts and they cannot get credit or charge cards. Other people don't want to have these types of accounts but they don't want to carry all of their money in cash and they want to buy things online.

To help these people, companies created prepaid cards. Most prepaid cards are used in many of the same places that credit and charge cards are used but instead of the company trusting you with their money, you deposit your money into an account (like a checking or saving account) and spend your own money.

Most companies that offer these cards will charge you a small fee to add your money to the account, about $5. Once the money is added to the card, you are able to spend it at stores and online but you don't receive a bill each month and you don't owe interest each month.

Before applying for a credit card, this may be a good type of card to start with, especially if you don't have a debit card, because it will allow you to practice managing a card account. If you add $50 to a prepaid card, you can only spend $50. It is very important that you don't lose your card (no matter what kind you have) because if someone finds it, they can spend your money. Also read the terms of agreement before signing up for one of these accounts so that you know what other fees you may be charged.

Which type of cards do you prefer… charge cards (pay all of the money back at the end of the month), credit cards (make payments each month plus interest), debit cards (spend money directly from your checking account) or prepaid cards (add cash to an account and spend only that amount)? _____

Why do you prefer this type of card?

_____

_____

_____

_____

MONTH	SUN	MON	TUES	WED	THURS	FRI	SAT

DATE	MONEY EARNED (INCOME)	HOW MUCH
		$
		$
		$
		$
TOTAL EARNED THIS WEEK		$

DATE	MONEY SPENT (EXPENSES)	HOW MUCH
	SAVE	$
		$
		$
		$
		$
		$
		$
		$
TOTAL SPENT THIS WEEK		$

I started this week with $_____

This week I should have $_____ **(started + earned – spent)**

WEEK 36

How can my money make money?

We've talked a lot about credit and spending money but let's get back to saving. By now, you know more about money than most young people and that's great! Let's keep going...

There are a few places other than a bank at home or a basic savings account that you can save money. One of the good things about using these other accounts is that they earn you interest. We have talked about paying interest to companies for money that we borrow but when we save our money in bank accounts such Money Market Accounts or Certificates of Deposit, the bank pays us interest!

These accounts don't earn a lot of interest but it is a good idea to understand how they work because as you continue to save, you will want your money to work as hard as you are working to earn it.

Check out the table below to see the difference between saving $100 in a piggy bank earning no interest, a savings account earning around 1% per month, a Money Market savings account earning around 2% per month and a Certificate of Deposit earning around 3% per month. (These percentages are examples and you need to check with your local bank about actual rates.)

	Piggy Bank			Savings Account			Money Market			Certificate of Deposit		
	Beg	+ 0%	= End	Beg	+ 1%	= End	Beg	+ 2%	= End	Beg	+ 3%	= End
Month 1	$100	$0	$100	$100	$1	$101	$100	$2	$102	$100	$3	$103
Month 2	$100	$0	$100	$101	$1	$102	$102	$2	$104	$103	$3	$106
Month 3	$100	$0	$100	$102	$1	$103	$104	$2	$106	$106	$3	$109
Month 4	$100	$0	$100	$103	$1	$104	$106	$2	$108	$109	$3	$112
Month 5	$100	$0	$100	$104	$1	$105	$108	$2	$110	$112	$3	$115
Month 6	$100	$0	$100	$105	$1	$106	$110	$2	$112	$115	$3	$118

MONTH	SUN	MON	TUES	WED	THURS	FRI	SAT

DATE	MONEY EARNED (INCOME)	HOW MUCH
		$
		$
		$
		$
TOTAL EARNED THIS WEEK		$

DATE	MONEY SPENT (EXPENSES)	HOW MUCH
	SAVE	$
		$
		$
		$
		$
		$
		$
		$
TOTAL SPENT THIS WEEK		$

I started this week with $_____

This week I should have $_____ (started + earned – spent)

WEEK 37

How can I prepare for my future?

Tomorrow is the biggest thief of our goals.

I hear so many people say that they are going to start doing this or start doing that… tomorrow. For many people, tomorrow never comes because they continue putting off their goals. So far, you have set some goals for your future and have a basic understanding of managing your money. What's next?

Let's look at a few strategies to help you achieve some of the goals that you have…

➢ **Never stop learning.** The more you learn, the more you can earn. We learned earlier that many jobs will pay you based on your education and experience. Once you receive a college degree (if you choose that route) there are more educational opportunities that you can pursue to enhance your resume. They include graduate school and specialized certificates.

➢ **If you are the smartest person in your crew, you need a new crew.** You should aspire to hang out with people that you can learn from. I'm not saying get rid of your friends that you grew up with and have been with you since kindergarten but as you imagine the life you want to have; you need to find people who have similar ambitions because they will help to encourage you to pursue your goals.

➢ **Don't be afraid to fail.** Sometimes when we dream big, we start to think of all of the things that can go wrong. I wish I could tell you that those things won't ever happen but they will. There are some things that you will want like nothing you have ever wanted in your life and you won't get it. People don't help us by making us believe that we will get everything that we want in life because it isn't true. The key is we can't be afraid to try and accept that we will succeed at some things and others we won't. When things don't work out, you have to learn the lesson from the experience.

➢ **Always think positive.** Life is going to throw you lemons (bad things happening). You will have two choices – suck on the lemons (focus on the negative) or make lemonade (find the positive). It won't always be easy but happiness is a choice. You can choose to focus on the negative or find the positive in whatever situation you find yourself in.

➢ **Be prepared.** Most opportunities come as a result of preparation. No matter what you do, you should always be prepared and be prepared to be the best. If I know I have to make a presentation, I research and practice because I want to be the best. If you are known as a person who is always prepared, you will be amazed at how many doors will open for you.

MONTH	SUN	MON	TUES	WED	THURS	FRI	SAT

DATE	MONEY EARNED (INCOME)		HOW MUCH
			$
			$
			$
			$
TOTAL EARNED THIS WEEK			$

DATE	MONEY SPENT (EXPENSES)		HOW MUCH
	SAVE		$
			$
			$
			$
			$
			$
			$
			$
TOTAL SPENT THIS WEEK			$

➢
➢ **I started this week with $_____**

➢ **This week I should have $_____ (started + earned – spent)**

WEEK 38

Money break…

How are you doing with your budget?

_____

_____

_____

_____

What is the most important thing that you have learned about money?

_____

_____

_____

_____

MONTH	SUN	MON	TUES	WED	THURS	FRI	SAT

DATE	MONEY EARNED (INCOME)	HOW MUCH
		$
		$
		$
		$
TOTAL EARNED THIS WEEK		$

DATE	MONEY SPENT (EXPENSES)	HOW MUCH
	SAVE	$
		$
		$
		$
		$
		$
		$
		$
TOTAL SPENT THIS WEEK		$

I started this week with $_____

This week I should have $_____ **(started + earned – spent)**

WEEK 39

Let's check on your SMART goals. How are you doing with them?

Money Goal _____

_____

_____

_____

_____

Goal #1 _____

_____

_____

_____

_____

Goal #2 _____

_____

_____

_____

_____

MONTH	SUN	MON	TUES	WED	THURS	FRI	SAT

DATE	MONEY EARNED (INCOME)					HOW MUCH	
						$	
						$	
						$	
						$	
TOTAL EARNED THIS WEEK						$	

DATE	MONEY SPENT (EXPENSES)					HOW MUCH	
	SAVE					$	
						$	
						$	
						$	
						$	
						$	
						$	
						$	
TOTAL SPENT THIS WEEK						$	

I started this week with $_____

This week I should have $_____ (started + earned – spent)

YOU HAVE JUST COMPLETED PART THREE OF YOUR MONEY MATTERS

LET'S CHECK ON YOUR MONEY MATTERS…

At the beginning of week 27, I had $_____

Between weeks 27 and 39, I earned $_____

Between weeks 27 and 39, I spent $_____

I should have (had + earned – spent) $_____

I have saved $_____

	Amount I had at the beginning …	Total amount earned…	Total amount spent…	Amount I should have…	Amount Saved…
Weeks 1-13		+	-	=	
Weeks 14-26		+	-	=	+
Weeks 27-39		+	-	=	+
Total					=

THE GOAL IN THIS SECTION WAS TO TEACH YOU SOME BASIC FINANCIAL TERMS

BREIFLY DESCRIBE HOW YOU WILL USE CREDIT IN YOUR FUTURE

_____

_____

_____

_____

_____

_____

_____

WEEK 40

What is investing?

When people want to save money for a long term goal (usually more than five years away), they invest their money into accounts that they hope will pay them more money than if they put it in a bank account. This is called investing.

Check out these 15 common investment terms…

Annual Percentage Rate (APR) – the interest rate based on the cost of credit in one year to pay for the money you borrow, based on compounding

Annual Percentage Yield (APY) – the interest rate earned or paid in one year, based on compounding

Appreciation – an increase in value of an asset such as a stock, bond or real estate

Ask price – the lowest price a seller will accept for a security

Assets – things you own, such as cash, real estate, stocks and bonds

Average annual return – the increased value of an investment, taking into account compounding

Basis – the price you paid for an investment when you bought it

Bear market – a market that is declining over several months or longer

Bid – the highest price that a potential buyer is willing to pay for a security

Bond – a security that pays a fixed amount of interest at a regular interval over a certain period with the promise to repay an amount on a certain date

Bull market – a market in which the prices (investments) are rising for several months

Capital gain – the difference between an asset's purchase price and selling price (if you buy 100 shares of stock at $20 per share and sell them for $30 per share, your capital gain is $1,000 [(100 x $30 = $3,000) – (100 x $20 = $2,000)]

Capital loss – the loss an investor suffers after selling an asset

Cash flow – the flow of money coming in and going out, positive means you don't spend more than you earn, negative means you are in debt

Diversification – spreading your risk among a variety of different types of investments such as stocks, bonds, real estate and cash

Don't try to memorize these terms. You can look back at them as we move forward.

MONTH	SUN	MON	TUES	WED	THURS	FRI	SAT

DATE	MONEY EARNED (INCOME)		HOW MUCH
			$
			$
			$
			$
TOTAL EARNED THIS WEEK			$

DATE	MONEY SPENT (EXPENSES)		HOW MUCH
	SAVE		$
			$
			$
			$
			$
			$
			$
			$
TOTAL SPENT THIS WEEK			$

I started this week with $_____

This week I should have $_____ (started + earned – spent)

WEEK 41

Let's go over 20 more common investing terms that will help you to understand some of things we will talk about later in this section...

Compound interest – interest earned on the principal amount (initial amount) and any interest already accrued

Dividend – money or stock that a corporation pays to its shareholders quarterly

Equity – the part of your ownership in something

52-week range – the highest and lowest price a security reached during the past year

Growth rate – the rate that stocks, the economy or earnings grow

Inflation – a rise in the prices of goods and services

Initial Price Offering (IPO) – the cost of a stock the first time it is made for sale to the public

Interest – the cost of borrowing money

Liability – legal obligations to pay for things you own

Mutual fund – an investment company that pools investors' money to invest in a variety of stocks, bonds and/or other securities

Net worth – the difference between your assets (what you own) and your liabilities (what you owe)

Portfolio – your combined investments including cash, bonds, stocks, mutual funds and real estate

Prime rate – the interest rate that banks use to price loans

Principal – the initial amount of money placed into an investment or if you are borrowing money, the total amount that is borrowed

Return of capital – money paid to you on the money you invested

Risk – the possibility that you could lose money on an investment

Securities – a general term used for stocks and bonds

Share price – the price of a unit of ownership in a company (stock) or mutual fund

Ticker symbol – a letter combination that uniquely identifies a stock

Withholding – the money deducted from your paycheck to pay state and federal taxes and insurances

MONTH	SUN	MON	TUES	WED	THURS	FRI	SAT

DATE	MONEY EARNED (INCOME)	HOW MUCH
		$
		$
		$
		$
TOTAL EARNED THIS WEEK		$

DATE	MONEY SPENT (EXPENSES)	HOW MUCH
	SAVE	$
		$
		$
		$
		$
		$
		$
		$
TOTAL SPENT THIS WEEK		$

I started this week with $_____

This week I should have $_____ (started + earned – spent)

WEEK 42

What is the difference between saving and investing?

Saving and investing are similar because in both situations you are setting aside money for a future purpose.

Saving is more of a sure thing. Most savings accounts, except your bank at home, are protected by the Federal Government so you are pretty sure that if you put your money into the account, the money will be there when you go to take it out.

Investing, on the other, involves risk. Risk is the possibility that something could go wrong. When you ride a bicycle, you are taking a risk that you could hurt yourself so you try to protect yourself from that risk by wearing a helmet and not going too fast. People who invest their money take a risk because they are giving a company money and hoping that the company makes money and pays you some of that money. If the company does not do well, you could lose your money and the company would not have to pay you back because you took a risk.

Good investments usually grow at a much faster rate than savings accounts because of the risk. The company is compensating you for trusting them and taking the risk.

How do you feel about risk? Would you prefer to save $100 and know how much money you will have at the end of ten years or invest $100 hoping to have $1,000 at the end of ten years but not knowing for sure?

_____

_____

_____

_____

MONTH	SUN	MON	TUES	WED	THURS	FRI	SAT

DATE	MONEY EARNED (INCOME)					HOW MUCH	
						$	
						$	
						$	
						$	
TOTAL EARNED THIS WEEK						$	

DATE	MONEY SPENT (EXPENSES)					HOW MUCH	
	SAVE					$	
						$	
						$	
						$	
						$	
						$	
						$	
						$	
TOTAL SPENT THIS WEEK						$	

I started this week with $_____

This week I should have $_____ (started + earned – spent)

WEEK 43

Why do I need to save and invest?

One of the terms that we learned a couple of weeks ago is 'diversification'. It is important for you to plan to have money in a few different baskets so that your money is always doing well.

Savings accounts like Money Markets and CDs are constant. They generate about the same amount of interest regardless of how the economy is doing.

Stocks, your investment in a particular company, do well when the company is doing well and usually the economy. When you buy a stock, you are buying a piece of a company. When the company is doing well then your stock will do well. As long as people have money to buy the company's products or services then they make money. When the economy is not doing well and people don't have money to buy the company's products/services then the company may not do well.

Bonds, on the other hand, usually do well when the economy isn't doing well or to fund major projects. Bonds are loans given to companies and parts of government with the promise that they will pay the money back. When you buy a bond, you are usually buying a piece of that loan and receiving a portion of the interest that they pay back. Most companies and parts of government only need to borrow money when the economy is not doing well and they are not making enough money to pay their bills.

Do you see why it is important to diversify your investment?

_____

_____

_____

_____

_____

MONTH	SUN	MON	TUES	WED	THURS	FRI	SAT

DATE	MONEY EARNED (INCOME)	HOW MUCH
		$
		$
		$
		$
TOTAL EARNED THIS WEEK		$

DATE	MONEY SPENT (EXPENSES)	HOW MUCH
	SAVE	$
		$
		$
		$
		$
		$
		$
		$
TOTAL SPENT THIS WEEK		$

I started this week with $_____

This week I should have $_____ (started + earned – spent)

WEEK 44

Let's pick some stocks…

Our society thrives on consumers. The economy grows when we buy things from companies. However, people thrive when they invest. Rather than only looking at companies and the things you can buy from them, consider investing in companies so that you can make money from the stuff other people buy. Before you start investing, you should understand a little bit about how stocks work. Over the next couple of weeks, we will check out some stocks.

Think about a company you buy stuff from – Wal-Mart, Target, Eastbay, Toys R Us, Nike – and get the following stock information about them.

Example   Yahoo! Inc.   Ticker or Symbol   YHOO

Today's Open Price (June 21, 2012) $15.73

I could buy 6 shares ($100/ $15.73 = 6.357 – always round down) for $94.38 ($15.73 x 6)

52 Week High - $16.79   My 6 shares would be worth $100.74 ($16.79 x 6 shares)

52 Week Low - $11.09   My 6 shares would be worth $66.54 ($11.09 x 6 shares)

After spending $94.38 on my 6 shares, I have to decide if I am willing to risk $27.84 ($94.38-$66.54) for the possibility of making $6.36 ($100.74-$94.38)

Company #1 _____Ticker or Symbol _____

Today's Open Price $_____How many shares could you buy with $100 _____

52 Week High $_____

How much would your shares be worth based on the 52 Week High $_____

52 Week Low $_____

How much would your shares be worth based on the 52 Week Low $_____

Is this a good investment? _____

MONTH	SUN	MON	TUES	WED	THURS	FRI	SAT

DATE	MONEY EARNED (INCOME)	HOW MUCH
		$
		$
		$
		$
TOTAL EARNED THIS WEEK		$

DATE	MONEY SPENT (EXPENSES)	HOW MUCH
	SAVE	$
		$
		$
		$
		$
		$
		$
		$
TOTAL SPENT THIS WEEK		$

I started this week with $_____

This week I should have $_____ (started + earned – spent)

WEEK 45

Let's pick another stock…

Company #2 _____Ticker or Symbol _____

Today's Open Price $_____How many shares could you buy with $100 _____

52 Week High $_____

How much would your shares be worth based on the 52 Week High $_____

52 Week Low $_____

How much would your shares be worth based on the 52 Week Low $_____

Is this a good investment? _____

How do you feel about investing so far?

_____

_____

_____

_____

Why do you think more people don't invest?

_____

_____

_____

_____

MONTH	SUN	MON	TUES	WED	THURS	FRI	SAT

DATE	MONEY EARNED (INCOME)	HOW MUCH
		$
		$
		$
		$
TOTAL EARNED THIS WEEK		$

DATE	MONEY SPENT (EXPENSES)	HOW MUCH
	SAVE	$
		$
		$
		$
		$
		$
		$
		$
TOTAL SPENT THIS WEEK		$

I started this week with $_____

This week I should have $_____ (started + earned – spent)

WEEK 46

Let's pick another stock…

Company #3 _____Ticker or Symbol _____

Today's Open Price $_____How many shares could you buy with $100 _____

52 Week High $_____

How much would your shares be worth based on the 52 Week High $_____

52 Week Low $_____

How much would your shares be worth based on the 52 Week Low $_____

Is this a good investment? _____

Based on the information you have learned so far, do you prefer to save at a bank or to invest in the stock market?

_____

_____

_____

Do you plan to make stocks a part of your future financial plan?

_____

_____

_____

_____

MONTH	SUN	MON	TUES	WED	THURS	FRI	SAT

DATE	MONEY EARNED (INCOME)	HOW MUCH
		$
		$
		$
		$
TOTAL EARNED THIS WEEK		$

DATE	MONEY SPENT (EXPENSES)	HOW MUCH
	SAVE	$
		$
		$
		$
		$
		$
		$
		$
TOTAL SPENT THIS WEEK		$

I started this week with $_____

This week I should have $_____ (started + earned – spent)

WEEK 47

What is my net worth?

As you get older, one of your goals should be to have a positive net worth. Your net worth is…

Assets (everything that you own)

- <u>Liabilities (everything you owe)</u>

Net Worth

Most Americans have a negative Net Worth because they owe more than they own. They are in debt. One of the goals of this workbook is to teach you how to focus on building assets and not creating a lot of debt.

Let's take a second to calculate your net worth. If you are in school and have student loans you should list them, even if you are not repaying them right now, they are still considered a liability.

How much money do you have? $_____

- How much money do you owe? $_____

My Net Worth is $_____

What are some ways that you can build a positive net worth?

_____

_____

_____

MONTH	SUN	MON	TUES	WED	THURS	FRI	SAT

DATE	MONEY EARNED (INCOME)	HOW MUCH
		$
		$
		$
		$
TOTAL EARNED THIS WEEK		$

DATE	MONEY SPENT (EXPENSES)	HOW MUCH
	SAVE	$
		$
		$
		$
		$
		$
		$
		$
TOTAL SPENT THIS WEEK		$

I started this week with $_____

This week I should have $_____ (started + earned – spent)

WEEK 48

Money Break…

There are a few things that you need to know about investing.

- ❖ **There is significant risk involved in investing in the stock market.** There are some people who have lost everything that they have saved in the stock market because they made bad investments. That is why it is very important that you diversify.
- ❖ **Investing is a long term strategy.** There are no get rich quick investments. If it sounds too good to be true then it probably is. Just as it takes time to make money, it will take time to grow your money.
- ❖ **Get everything in writing.** Whenever you give someone money, for any reason, get it in writing. It does not matter if you are loaning someone money or investing money, you should get a written agreement that at least includes both of your names, the date, the amount received, the amount agreed to be returned and terms of the agreement.
- ❖ **It costs money to invest.** There are fees that must be paid when you buy and sell stocks and bonds. Anyone buying investments under the age of 18 will need to have an adult to assist them. It would be wise to visit a licensed financial advisor before making a purchase or sale. Although there are online sites that allow you to manage investments, I recommend that you work with a professional.
- ❖ **Always check your numbers.** Math is a very important tool when managing your money. Don't just take people's word for things. Double check their numbers so that you can be sure you understand what is happening with your money. If you don't understand something, keep asking until you do – YOUR MONEY MATTERS!
- ❖ **Check your accounts once per quarter.** This book is divided into four sections or quarters. A quarter in a year is thirteen weeks or approximately three months. Banks normally send statements every month while most investment firms will send them quarterly. Don't take for granted that everything is ok, look over the statements and make sure the information is correct.
- ❖ **Some accounts may charge you to withdraw your money.** I know that sounds kind of odd because it's your money but banks make money off of your money and when they don't have your money, they can't make money. Therefore, they may charge you if you withdraw your money from a Certificate of Deposit before a certain date or if you make too many withdrawals from a Money Market. Before depositing or investing your money, ask about the fees that go with the account.

MONTH	SUN	MON	TUES	WED	THURS	FRI	SAT

DATE	MONEY EARNED (INCOME)	HOW MUCH
		$
		$
		$
		$
TOTAL EARNED THIS WEEK		$

DATE	MONEY SPENT (EXPENSES)	HOW MUCH
	SAVE	$
		$
		$
		$
		$
		$
		$
		$
TOTAL SPENT THIS WEEK		$

- ❖
- ❖ **I started this week with $_____**

- ❖ **This week I should have $_____ (started + earned – spent)**

WEEK 49

Sharing is caring…

I hope that you are not only learning a lot about your money matters but also sharing what you know. This week I want you to pick five things that you have learned so far and pick five different people to share the information with.

Lesson #1 _____

_____

I will share with _____

Lesson #2 _____

_____

I will share with _____

Lesson #3 _____

_____

I will share with _____

Lesson #4 _____

_____

I will share with _____

Lesson #5 _____

_____

I will share with _____

MONTH	SUN	MON	TUES	WED	THURS	FRI	SAT

DATE	MONEY EARNED (INCOME)	HOW MUCH
		$
		$
		$
		$
TOTAL EARNED THIS WEEK		$

DATE	MONEY SPENT (EXPENSES)	HOW MUCH
	SAVE	$
		$
		$
		$
		$
		$
		$
TOTAL SPENT THIS WEEK		$

I started this week with $_____

This week I should have $_____ (started + earned – spent)

WEEK 50

It's time to plan for next year!

Your money matters and you need to order your money management workbook for next year…

Make sure you check for Volume 2 because it will have new information for each week so that you can continue building on what you have already learned.

Bonus… I'm sure there is someone that you know who needs help with their money matters, order them a workbook also as your good deed for this week.

If you order them this week, they should arrive before you finish this workbook and you won't miss a week.

MY MONEY MATTERS

MONTH	SUN	MON	TUES	WED	THURS	FRI	SAT

DATE	MONEY EARNED (INCOME)	HOW MUCH
		$
		$
		$
		$
TOTAL EARNED THIS WEEK		$

DATE	MONEY SPENT (EXPENSES)	HOW MUCH
	SAVE	$
		$
		$
		$
		$
		$
		$
		$
TOTAL SPENT THIS WEEK		$

I started this week with $_____

This week I should have $_____ **(started + earned – spent)**

WEEK 51

It's a been a few weeks since you picked your stocks, let's take a look and see how they are doing…

Stock #1

_____

Purchased at $ _____

Today's Price $ _____

Stock #2

_____

Purchased at $ _____

Today's Price $ _____

Stock #3

_____

Purchased at $ _____

Today's Price $ _____

MY MONEY MATTERS

MONTH	SUN	MON	TUES	WED	THURS	FRI	SAT

DATE	MONEY EARNED (INCOME)					HOW MUCH	
						$	
						$	
						$	
						$	
TOTAL EARNED THIS WEEK						$	

DATE	MONEY SPENT (EXPENSES)					HOW MUCH	
	SAVE					$	
						$	
						$	
						$	
						$	
						$	
						$	
						$	
TOTAL SPENT THIS WEEK						$	

I started this week with $_____

This week I should have $_____ (started + earned – spent)

WEEK 52

Let's take a final look at your SMART goals…

Money Goal _____

_____

_____

_____

Goal #1 _____

_____

_____

_____

Goal #2 _____

_____

_____

_____

MONTH	SUN	MON	TUES	WED	THURS	FRI	SAT

DATE	MONEY EARNED (INCOME)	HOW MUCH
		$
		$
		$
		$
TOTAL EARNED THIS WEEK		$

DATE	MONEY SPENT (EXPENSES)	HOW MUCH
	SAVE	$
		$
		$
		$
		$
		$
		$
		$
TOTAL SPENT THIS WEEK		$

I started this week with $_____

This week I should have $_____ (started + earned – spent)

CONGRATULATIONS!!

YOU HAVE JUST COMPLETED PART FOUR OF YOUR MONEY MATTERS

AND THE WORKBOOK FOR AN ENTIRE YEAR!!

LET'S CHECK ON YOUR MONEY MATTERS…

At the beginning of week 40, I had $_____

Between weeks 40 and 52, I earned $_____

Between weeks 40 and 52, I spent $_____

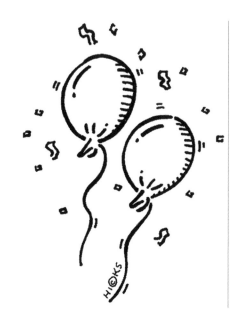

I should have (had + earned – spent) $_____

I have saved $_____

	Amount I had at the beginning …	Total amount earned…	Total amount spent…	Amount I should have…	Amount Saved…
Weeks 1-13		+	-	=	
Weeks 14-26		+	-	=	+
Weeks 27-39		+	-	=	+
Weeks 40-52		+	-	=	+
Total					=

THE GOAL IN THIS SECTION WAS TO TEACH YOU ABOUT INVESTING

BREIFLY DESCRIBE HOW INVESTING WILL HELP YOU REACH YOUR FINANCIAL GOALS

_____

_____

_____

_____

_____

_____

THANK YOU FOR TAKING THIS JOURNEY!

After 52 weeks, I hope you have learned why YOUR MONEY MATTERS and some financial management tools that will help you to be successful in whatever you do with your life…

SHARE WITH ME WHY YOUR MONEY MATTERS…

Email me: CONTACT@LAKESHAWOMACK.COM

Tweet me: @LAKESHAWOMACK using #MyMoneyMatters

Post on Facebook: FACEBOOK.COM/MyMoneyMattersWorkbooks

Mail it to me at: PO BOX 900, EVERGREEN, AL 36401

ABOUT THE AUTHOR

LaKesha Womack worked as a licensed Financial Advisor for a reputable Financial Services Corporation that has been providing American families with financial planning information for hundreds of years. While studying for her securities license, LaKesha became amazed at the amount of information about investing, money management and financial planning that the average American was unaware of. Since leaving the financial services industry, LaKesha has worked as a Business Consultant for her firm, Womack Consulting Group, helping entrepreneurs in various industries to start and grow a small business.

She continues to provide financial guidance on her blogs (LaKeshaWomack.com and WomackCG.com), in seminars and workshops as well as through peer to peer consultations. Although LaKesha is no longer able to buy and sell financial securities and insurance products, she believes that the knowledge she has should be shared with others who have a desire to make better financial decisions.

LaKesha is the author of "Building a Brand without Spending a Bundle", "Success Secrets for the Young & Fabulous" and "Is She The ONE?" with additional projects in progress. She lives in her hometown of Evergreen, Alabama where she is raising her young son and teaching him about money using the Basic Money Management Principle.

Made in the USA
Lexington, KY
25 May 2013